Have you just been made the boss? Appointed the new leader of a business, or a business like organisation?

Congratulations. *This book is for you. To help you be the very best leader you can be. From day 1. Because what you do on day 1, week 1 and month 1 and indeed your first 100 days will be critical to your success long term.*

So what do you do in that critical first period?

If you have an MBA and have trained to lead a business. Great! Hopefully you know exactly what you're doing and this book is redundant. Although I suspect not as most of what is in here is not stuff they teach you on an MBA course. Instead it draws on my experience as a General Manager, Managing Director and twice Chief Executive, as well as my experience on the receiving end of at least two new bosses myself.

If you haven't got an MBA, don't worry! I have been working with SME Managing Directors for over two decades and a big revelation for me is that most did not set out to run a business. They are an ***accidental business leader.*** *That in itself is NOT the problem – many entrepreneurial people do a great job; indeed usually better than those bogged down in theory!*

It is though a reason new business leaders sometimes feel like Imposters. They feel slightly insecure having to pretend to everyone they're fully in control when in reality they're busking it.

Whatever your background and training this book is for you. Not as a rulebook you should follow slavishly as every situation is different, but as food for thought to help you be an even better leader and achieve even more success for your business!

More thoughts, tips and tools on business leadership available at:
www.BobOnBusiness.co.uk
www.Leadership-Strategy-Growth.co.uk
blog.BobBradley.co.uk

More books on business leadership available at:
www.BobOnBusiness.co.uk/Books
www.BobOnBusiness.co.uk/eBooks

This book (book zero) available at:
www.BobOnBusiness.co.uk/Book0
www.BobOnBusiness.co.uk/eBook0

Author contact details
www.BobBradley.co.uk/contact
www.LinkedIn.com/in/BobBradley
Email: Bob@BobBradley.co.uk

This book like most others could not have been produced without the really valuable contributions of a whole team of people.

I'd first like to thank everyone that has ever helped me in business or inspired me. That includes my former managers as well as some great people in my many teams.

My good friend the very experienced Sir Eric Peacock talks about a thirst for learning and "stealing with pride" and there is no doubt I have taken that to heart as nothing in this book is magic. It's all simple common sense stuff that I've picked up, mainly from other people, over the years.

Specific thanks must however go first and foremost to Sam Ellis, my shadow who's taken my words and somehow made them look good as well as doing masses to raise my profile on LinkedIn and elsewhere.

And I'm also so grateful for all the reviews and detailed feedback I've received from so many directions including Frank Nigrello, Ned Wells, Robyn Pearce, David Hummel-Newell, Laura Bradley, John Cardy, Gareth Chick, Wendy Marks, Martin Craven and everyone else whose names I've forgotten to include! Your efforts have not gone unnoticed!

First published in Great Britain in 2024

Paperback: ISBN: 978-1-0687476-0-1
eBook: ASIN: B0DHSS87MT

Contents

6 key challenges facing the new CEO

To succeed the new CEO has to accurately balance a lot of competing pressures of which the following are key:

1. How much to listen and how much to decide based on your own research, experience and instinct
2. Who really has what power? Who must you have on-side for your big decisions? Which are the critical battles you need to fight and win now?
3. What is rightly done the way it is because of real past organisational learning and what is unjustified legacy that you need to fix?
4. What are the important things you need to get right and what are less important imperfections and niggles that you can ignore - at least for now?
5. What resources (primarily people, money and time) do you need and when? How do you ensure you have sufficient of them to achieve what you need to when you need to?
6. How quickly do you need to change what? What do you need to address quickly and what can you defer?

23 tips for the new leader

Overall

1. Listen and learn then plan then act.
2. Make haste slowly. Act quickly but gather information and check the reality enough before acting.
3. Signal values and expectations clearly. Don't act too early in your enthusiasm to demonstrate impact.

Gather information

4 Ensure you understand just why you were appointed and check in with stakeholders carefully before rolling out your plan.

5 Meet all staff one way or another. Watch the teams in action, maybe even have a go yourself. Check out how everyone feels about the things. Listen and build relationships but be clear that to listen does not mean to accept and agree. Consider the informal as well as the formal relationships.

6 Meet and understand customers and suppliers and understand the internal perceptions of them.

7 Understand the business processes and especially most critical core business process. The process from suppliers through operations to customers and especially the customer journey.

Plan and decide

8 Reflect and learn. Be sure you understand exactly how the business really works.

9 What is the fundamental purpose of the business. Why does it need to exist? What problems does the business solve? For whom exactly? Focus is critical to success and purpose is critical to motivation (as well as recruitment and retention) in today's world.

10 Identify a strategy for success that makes sure your business is in the right place at the right time.

11 What culture is needed to fit the strategy? What are the unwritten ground rules (How things are done around here / What happens when you're not in the room.) What should they be? Make them explicit.

12 Which processes are critical to the success of the organisation. Look for tactical quick wins as well as strategic opportunities to improve.

13 What organisation structure is needed? If change is likely, begin with the end in mind. What is the perfect structure? Then work back from there taking into account who is in what roles now. Role clarity is important. Define roles by outcomes, not activity.

Plan and decide

14 How should the organisation communicate? It is important to communicate well but meetings are costly so ensure there is a structure for communication and specifically that all meetings have a clear purpose.

15 What change projects are needed? Projects are your key tool for performance improvement but require focus, commitment and time. So do fewer better! Ready, fire aim! It's progress, not perfection. Make haste slowly. Plan using a rolling wave. Pause and think carefully before releasing your plan.

16 Take risks but not unnecessary ones. When you're driving a lot of change it may be worth deferring decisions where there is an imbalanced impact from a balanced decision. One where a decision is 50:50 and the upside is useful but insignificant whilst the downside risk is serious.

Launch

17 Plan the launch sequence carefully. Ensure support of the key players, internal and external, before launch.

18 On launch, ensure clear and timely communication to all relevant parties.

19 Manage the difficult stuff carefully. Your responsibility is to be respected, not necessarily liked or agreed with. Be open and straightforward. Acknowledge the pain.

20 Share the strategy and purpose clearly and positively with continuing staff. Be positive about those leaving. It's not their fault. The decisions are to protect and build the future business. Unite the team behind messages that will stand the test of time.

21 Manage the projects, processes and systems. Create a sense of urgency and build credibility by delivering quick wins and celebrating them.

22 Fine tune as you proceed by including review and learning processes. Make change normal.

23 Look after yourself too. The business can't succeed without you taking the time to think clearly and behave rationally.

First thoughts
Why do the first 100 days matter?

Introduction

So you've just been appointed the new leader of your organisation. You are now the Managing Director, the Chief Executive, the Senior Partner, or simply the boss.

What do you do now? Drawing on my experience as a General Manager, Managing Director and twice Chief Executive, as well as my experience on the receiving end of at least two new bosses and observing what they did right and what I think they did wrong, I offer you my advice.

The astute reader will have noted that in the previous paragraph I humbly use the word 'think' to describe what they did wrong. Sadly that's just me being modest. The word should be 'know' as in both cases the business they took on did not exist five years later, at least not as an independent entity.

I say that with sadness, not with pleasure, as both were great businesses on an upward trajectory when they took on the role of leader.

I mention those two case studies at the start of this book because they reinforce both the level of impact great and poor leadership can have and also because there was a commonality in what went wrong in both cases. A commonality that reflects a pattern I have seen elsewhere since and which I will address first.

Listen and learn, plan and act

In these two cases, and others I have observed from the outside, the mistake was simple: The new leader knew what worked for them before and they deployed the same strategy in their new business with insufficient understanding of the differences in that business, even though they appeared to be similar businesses operating in a similar market.

The details of why they went wrong differed. In my first case it was the leader's failure to understand why the sales model they had inherited worked well with the buying patterns of the customers that business served. Restructuring sales to match the way they did it in their previous business severely damaged revenues.

In my second case it was the investors that mattered. Investors had backed the business for medium term strategic growth as a market consolidation play. The new leader decided to drive short term profit and cancel strategic investments and acquisitions.

Great! The company made short term profits but within three years investors lost patience with the lack of strategic growth and accepted an offer from a competitor to be consolidated rather than be the consolidator as was the original plan.

TIPS & TRICKS

No two businesses, even direct competitors in the same industry, are ever the same. They may have different ownership, structures, ambitions, leadership and most importantly cultures and market position. Think of RyanAir, EasyJet and British Airways.

Global best practice

A good starting point is to consider how one of the world's most powerful leaders behaves. When a new US President is inaugurated, there is much monitoring of their 'First 100 days'. And there is a good reason for that. Whether we like it or not, the signals a leader transmits, whether knowingly or inadvertently, are always important. Especially so in the first period for the new leader. The perceptions of people as to the nature of the leader can influence results for a long time and once established are very difficult to change.

Image: www.unsplash.com: sbranch

Experienced teachers signal expectations clearly

A well-understood illustration of that, because we were all students once, comes from the teaching profession.

A well understood illustration of the importance of signals comes from the teaching profession.

If you were an experienced teacher you'd know how critical it is to establish the right relationship with your class from the outset. So you would deliberately take a very firm line at first.

Once your ability to control the class is established, there is then room for flexibility to be introduced. The class knows you are in control and you can take control if necessary

TIPS & TRICKS

Use your first meeting to set the tone of your leadership. Signal your style and that you are engaging and open but in control.

This is a far better scenario than if you had begun softly, and the class gained the view that they can do what they want. And then it seems no amount of strictness, shouting or otherwise can regain control.

Image: www.canva.com

The core challenge - To make haste - slowly!

The challenge facing you, as the new leader, is balancing two competing demands. The need to really understand the company and decide your strategy and plan before making key decisions and sending signals must be balanced with the need to demonstrate progress and elevate the organisation's performance.

The appointment of a new leader usually creates an expectation, and an opportunity, for change. An opportunity you shouldn't miss. But it is important to get that change right. There is nothing worse than a visible strategic mistake in the early days for demolishing a new leader's credibility – forever!

On the other hand if action is left too long, people will conclude that things are going to continue as they were and the opportunity will have been missed. 3 months or 100 days seems from experience to be a good guideline as to the critical period during which a new leader needs to both learn enough to make good decisions and do enough to effectively set the direction for the future.

The rolling wave

So having explained the importance of the first 100 days, I'm now going to dismiss it and suggest that in my experience, whilst the 100 day milestone is the most important, it is wise for a new leader to have a clear understanding about how they are going to focus their activity for the first week, the first month, the first quarter (90 to 100 days) and the first year. And at each stage to develop the plan for the next, longer stage.

And to be clear those timescales are of course approximate - there is nothing magic about a calendar week or a calendar month. They are simply implying a short term focus moving step by step to the longer term. The exact lengths may be compressed if you are dealing with a crisis or extended if you are transforming step by step a business that is sustainably successful already.

TIPS & TRICKS

Avoid thinking things will be perfect tomorrow. Celebrate quick wins and make fast progress rather than striving endlessly for perfection.

The limitations of this book

TIPS & TRICKS

Challenge your assumptions. There is no single simple formula for success. If there was, your role wouldn't be so well paid! Every business is different. Don't assume that because an approach worked for you in a different business in the past it will work for you in this business today.

You will note as you read on, that this book starts with fairly detailed guidance and then as the book progresses and time passes becomes less detailed. That is deliberate and reflects the top tip I began this article with. I can give you precise tips as to what to do in the early stages because that is not specific to the business. You don't know the business any more than I do writing this book in abstract.

Actually that's not true. You will undoubtedly have gained a lot of information during your own recruitment process. My caution to you is not to assume that information is correct. Make sure you start out as a detective - gathering information, clues and evidence to try to work out the big picture based on motives, attitudes and behaviours.

TIPS & TRICKS

Don't assume the stakeholders know what they want and how to achieve it. It's obviously crucial to thoroughly understand and, if necessary, manage expectations on the results you can achieve. Additionally It's even more likely that they misunderstand the challenge on the ground. On balance most stakeholders should be flexible on how, if you are delivering the results they want.

It always amazes me how much my perception of a business changes as I peer beneath the covers. Businesses have an image to convey and protect, and the people putting you in place have perceptions of the challenge they are hiring you to deal with that may be misplaced or misguided. You are unlikely to succeed if you dive in based on either perception and take action without checking the reality on the ground.

Image: David Hyner - https://www.davidhyner.com

First week
Find your feet

TIPS & TRICKS

Start by focusing on yourself, your role, your priorities and your key people: Why are you there? Then send the right signals, listen and learn.

Set expectations around style and pace

Image: www.unsplash.com - Christine Donaldson

The priority for the first week must be to settle in. To find your desk, meet your immediate reports, explain to them your working style, your immediate priorities and maybe introduce yourself to all staff.

If you run an all hands 'town hall' meeting in the first weeks make sure you set the scene and their expectations carefully. You are going to listen before you decide and act. You want and value their input. They should not expect decisions until you have completed a review of the business. That will, for most, be somewhat reassuring.

Check the reality on the ground before acting

And the reality needs to be the same. Most leaders have a tendency to be decisive and take action. That's what makes them good leaders. But that's not right at this stage. Unless you have some previous insight or the organisation is in crisis, this is not a time for decisions – at least not for finally committing to them and communicating them.

TIPS & TRICKS

I find it helpful to be open in sharing what I see as my style of leadership from the start - as much as I understand it myself. So people know what to expect from me and how to manage me.

Listen and build relationships

Image: www.freepik.com

Decisions communicated within the first week run a high risk of being seen, probably accurately, as being made without proper consideration, without listening, without consulting and without due diligence. And however logical they may seem to an outsider (and the stakeholders) it is just possible that there are some good reasons, known only to insiders, as to why they are not good decisions.

The first week is though a good time to meet one or two key customers and suppliers to signal how important they are to your organisation, as well as get their input.

Again though, avoid making early commitments that you might later regret. Definitely listen to their thoughts, tell them you will take their views into account, and where appropriate you'll take quick simple actions to get minor issues resolved. Take care though to avoid committing to significant actions you don't know whether and how you can deliver.

Don't overreact in your enthusiasm to demonstrate impact

Most reasonable customers will understand that, however big the problem and however much you want to help, you don't, in any substantial organisation, have the ability to wave a magic wand and fix complex organisational challenges instantly. Hopefully they will accept and support your case that you need to build a solution that can be sustained and will lead to a permanent improvement in service, not a quick fix that falls away as quickly as it is implemented.

Check back: Just why were you appointed?

With all this in mind, the critical thing to establish is why you are there. Ask yourself, why have you been appointed?

What are the intentions of the stakeholders that appointed you? Is the business in crisis? Is this a turnaround situation? Is there a need to drive change but sort out an immediate crisis? Or is the need to sustain what's already going well and build on that?

How does everyone else feel about the situation?

Just as important; where do the people in the business feel they are? Do they feel the crisis behind your appointment or do they feel things are going well? Do they feel in crisis when the stakeholders feel all is ok? These dynamics and beliefs can help or hinder your ability to drive the business forward effectively.

The mistake for you as a new leader is to get into detail at this stage. Send signals and share your principles and values. Show you have a foundation and mean business but are wise enough not to come in with magic solutions. You want to listen and assess properly before you take clear actions and exhibit strong leadership.

Information gathering

As a new leader, you have a unique and one off opportunity to gain a comprehensive understanding of the business by learning how the organisation operates from the perspective of staff, customers, suppliers, and other stakeholders.

Image: www.freepik.com - rawpixel

Before making any major decisions, it is crucial to take advantage of this time to gather information. Additionally, this is a time when people will be patient with your decision-making process, and they will gladly provide you with a wealth of information to assist in decision-making. And that is something to be relished.

A one-off chance to get the truth

One of the challenges for you later, once you are an established leader, is that your established position, and the established perceptions of you, mean that no one will tell you the pure reality. It will inevitably be shaded by what the communicator feels the established leader wants, needs or ought to hear, coloured by their own agenda.

That is why consultants are often criticised for borrowing your watch to tell you the time. Having worked as a consultant myself, I'd say the adage is true. It is so easy. Staff are delighted to tell the consultant, or the new leader, the whole unvarnished truth in a way they won't tell an established incumbent.

Whether the established leader likes it and believes it, or not, they are nearly always told a story. People are 'economical with the truth'. Not outright lies obviously, just with a slant that reflects their own position - and yours.

Experienced leaders recognise that and often use intermediaries of some sort to get an objective indication of the truth.

TIPS & TRICKS

Use your newness to your advantage. Play dumb. Ask dumb questions. How does this work? Why do we do this? How do you feel about that?

Signal sending

Within the information gathering process you're unlikely to make key decisions or changes, but you should be sending signals about your style, values and priorities. The very act of listening before acting sends a signal. And so does the decision not to rush in with big decisions in month one.

They all signal a calm, controlled, rational leader. So don't be afraid to communicate and establish your leadership style early on. This can be beneficial in gaining support and building consensus as you move forward.

Image: www.unsplash.com - Chinh Le Duc

Action 1: Meet all staff

TIPS & TRICKS

The goal in this stage: Research perceptions of the business from all angles - 'Seek first to understand'.

Image: www.freepik.com - fabrikasimf

Meet all staff one way or another

One set of activities I recommend strongly in month one is meeting **all** staff individually, in small groups or as sample groups depending upon the scale of the organisation.

Get out and about. And I deliberately say all, meaning all available, staff as there is no doubt that one of the biggest motivators of staff is being asked their opinion and being listened to. For some of my favourite questions and tips for meeting staff visit appendix A.

To listen does not mean to agree

Listening definitely does not mean doing everything they say and that must be a clear part of the introduction to your conversation.

Giving staff of all levels a chance to contribute their thoughts is amazingly motivational.

Interestingly, sometimes the most powerful insights come from the most junior staff unhindered by the politics and diplomacy that often taints senior managerial input. Just make sure they understand you are listening not agreeing and will make a decision in due course.

Image: www.unsplash.com - Clement Falize

Reflect and learn

After your meetings, be sure to take some time to reflect on what your team said. What did you learn about your business?

As you work through these meetings develop hypotheses as to how the organisation really works. What's good and what's bad, where the opportunities are inside and out, and where the strategy, tactics, processes and systems are solid and where less so.

But don't leap to conclusions too quickly. Pause until you've got the full picture from all parts of the organisation. Remembering again that people have differing perspectives and will sell their story.

Consider individuals and the formal and informal relationships

Likewise as you get out and about, be thinking about who are the strong members of staff, who are the compliant passengers and who are disruptive, whether visibly or quietly.

Think about where the real power within the business sits. That may not be with the hierarchy. The reality of human relationships is that people form their own communities.

Power in an organisation can lie with people who have no formal authority. That might be those that meet in the smoking pod outside, or it could be the football team or any other group. If you are unconvinced, just talk to a prison officer, as I have recently, about where power really lies in a prison!

Month one: Weeks 2-4
Listen and learn

Action 2: Meet customers and suppliers

TIPS & TRICKS

Use this moment to build a personal and practical relationship, business leader to business leader, with most senior contact you can reach within your top customers.

Soon after your meetings with staff, once you have a bit of a handle on what the organisation does and how, but before you are bogged down in detail, it is critical to meet a range (at least a dozen) of top customers and suppliers. I recommend doing this both with staff alongside you so you can observe the nature of the relationship and also without so you can get honest feedback.

Again, while you are the new leader, suppliers and customers are likely to be more open about their true perceptions. So take the liberty of using your position as new to ask seemingly simple 'dumb' questions that established leaders may struggle with because, whether justifiably or not, they are often expected to possess complete knowledge of every critical relationship.

Meet and understand customers

Meeting with top customers gives you an opportunity to hear directly from them about their experiences with your company: What they like and don't like, and what they would like to see changed. By asking probing questions you will get a good understanding of your customers' needs and how you can better serve them.

This information will be invaluable as you work to grow your business and improve your products or services. Refer to appendix B for some of my favourite questions for customers and top tips for conducting customer interviews.

Image: www.freepik.com

How do customers perceive and position your business?

What did you learn about your business?

You will inevitably find out where your business is failing to meet expectations.

It is important for you to understand such perceptions and later address them properly if you are to be seen by customers as enhancing the position of your business as a supplier to them.

So take some time to reflect on what they said. Consider the perceptions, interests and behaviours of customers so that you can consider how the products or services your business supplies can better, and more profitably, meet your customers' needs.

That may mean adding features, products and services. Or, just as likely, there might be opportunities to drop features that cost the business a lot to provide and which are not really valued by the market.

It may even require big decisions to exit a market, tackle a new one or revise the product / service offer dramatically.

TIPS & TRICKS

The words 'later' and 'perceptions' are critical. Whilst obviously it's worth taking quick wins and fixing simple problems quickly to reinforce the relationship and show you mean business, it can be very dangerous for the new leader to return to the office and get staff to address customer criticisms quickly without also carefully considering the root cause of the dissatisfaction.

Without proper consideration and rectification of the business process that created the mismatched expectation in the first place, there is a risk of, whilst fixing that one-off problem, causing a bigger or repeated problem later or elsewhere. For example the root cause of a problem may not be the failure to fulfil a customer's expectations, but rather the expectations themselves that were established with the customer, which may not be viable for the business to service.

A second problem is the internal culture that could be created. A 'shoot from the hip, run around and do a quick fix to address a problem as a result of them escalating to the boss' culture isn't helpful. It's a sure fire way of ensuring more customers bring you more problems, more often, in future. You really don't need to be dragged into that!

Meet suppliers

Meeting with key suppliers is an essential step for any new business leader looking to get familiar with their company's operations. Suppliers can provide valuable insights into the strengths and weaknesses of your business, what you do well, and what you can improve upon.

In this section, and in appendix C, we will discuss the key questions to ask when meeting with key suppliers to gain an understanding of their perceptions of your business and to signal your interest in improving the commercial relationship by exploring how you can work together to optimise their price and service.

The term key suppliers certainly means the supply chain for your core product or service. Depending upon the nature of the business it can also mean for example your IT supplier (if the IT platform is critical to your business), your brand marketing and/or PR agencies, (if your market profile is especially critical), or your advertising/ lead generation agency (if you use them to create opportunities to grow your business).

All may have an insight on your business and the potential to improve your position.

How do suppliers perceive and position your business?

Finding out your company's strengths and weaknesses in dealing with them can provide valuable insights into areas of your business that could be improved.

Ask them to provide an industry view of the quality of your products and your level of customer service.

Image: www.freepik.com - Drazen Zigic

TIPS & TRICKS

Use these meetings to understand the industry. Suppliers are by definition likely to be in or close to your industry. They may also supply your competitors. Meeting them is also then a good chance to understand their perspective of your industry - and indeed you may even be able to get them to share their perceptions of how your business compares to your competitors. It's certainly useful to understand their view whether you take it at face value or not!

Look for opportunities - Tactical and strategic

Explore the potential to do more together. Understand their manufacturing and supply process and how it integrates into your own supply chain. Look at mutual performance metrics and lead times and get a sense of the supplier's capabilities and constraints.

How can you jointly streamline the supply chain processes to reduce the costs and delays in the overall supply chain? How can you improve communication? Listening to their feedback and acting on it can help build a stronger relationship and ultimately benefit your business.

Examine the strategic opportunities. How can you deliver more, better and more profitable products and services to your customers utilising their supply line. They may have ideas, such as offering custom solutions or introducing new product lines. By working together with your suppliers to improve their contribution to your own products or services, you may be able to gain a competitive advantage.

Overall, the goal is not to control the supplier, but to develop a cooperative relationship; one where both parties collaborate to promote the profitable growth of both businesses, through improving the supply chain as a whole. Taking the time to listen and understand their perspectives and needs will also help you build a solid and long-lasting business relationship.

Image: www.freepik.com - asier_relampago...

Action 3: Check in with stakeholders

TIPS & TRICKS

The goal in this stage: **Confirm why am I here?**

Once you've explored the perceptions and priorities of staff, customers and suppliers it is a good time for you to check (back) in with key stakeholders to reassess their priorities, now with the benefit of a good understanding of other perspectives.

This step should include engaging with shareholders, the board, and potentially other critical entities like banks or lenders that have a significant impact on the business.

By engaging in these conversations, armed with a deeper understanding of various perspectives, you can continue to clarify and confirm the underlying purpose of why you have been appointed and ensure that all stakeholders are aligned in achieving the overall objectives.

This reassessment will also show how you are proactive and adaptable in a dynamic business environment enabling you to stay ahead of the curve and meet the needs of all parties involved. For some of my favourite questions for bankers or investors refer to appendix D.

Image: www.unsplash.com - Amy Hirschi

Action 4: Understand how the business really works

So now you have a handle on the perceptions of key people: The internal perceptions of your own staff and the external perceptions of suppliers and customers.

I deliberately suggest you leave the next step until after you have solicited most or all of those perceptions so that you can gather those insights whilst being able to 'play dumb' in not knowing how products and services are (or are supposed to be) delivered.

Now though, before you come up with your plans for the future, it is critical to check out some of the practical stuff. The facts and figures and the fundamental core processes and systems of the business.

Critical facts and figures

It's pretty obvious that a key source of information to review is the financial information in the accounts. But do so with care. My very first MBA finance lecture was spent demonstrating to us how accounts can, completely legally, be adapted to convey very different impressions.

So don't just take the numbers as facts. Check out the assumptions, especially how revenue is recognised and how inventory is valued.

Most importantly examine the management accounts and understand how costs are allocated to product lines in directs or to overheads. Put simply try to get to grips with how profit is calculated and, separately, what drives it.

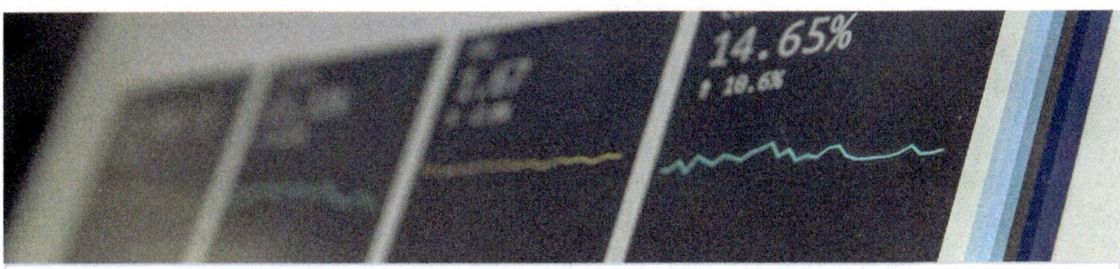

Image: www.unsplash.com - Stephen Dawson

Don't stop with the accounts though. Numerous other financial analyses can be useful. For example consider the concentration of revenues by account. Are most revenues coming from a small number of customers? And what about profit by account?

Often it is the second quartile of accounts that are most profitable. Typically the biggest customers negotiate the best discounts and are very demanding and the smallest customers are expensive to service relative to their revenue contribution. Generally revenues from a wide range of customers are more secure than revenues from a small customer set. But a small set of customers can be more profitable.

Likewise, consider the product groups. Are a small number of products responsible for most of the revenue? And profit?

Many businesses evolve over time to sell a wide range of products, many of which are no longer profitable to produce. At least in the volumes they are sold today. Whilst there is an argument that the full, broad product range is important for customers, the most profitable companies are often those that focus on a small niche.

The most critical process - the customer journey

The most important process in almost every business is the core business process or the customer journey. This process typically takes a prospect from being unaware of your business's existence to becoming aware, engaging, discussing specific opportunities, contracting with your business to address those opportunities, going through the implementation and delivery process, receiving post-sales support, and ultimately, making repeat purchases.

Essentially, this journey encompasses all touchpoints and experiences customers have with your business, from start to finish. Understanding and optimising this process is key to building a successful, sustainable business.

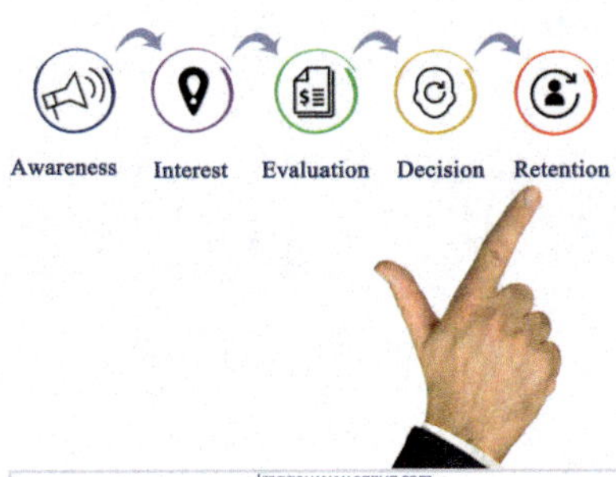

Image: www.canva.com

Watch the teams in action. Maybe even have a go yourself

I would especially recommend that, as part of your research, you listen in on a number of sales calls and/or join a number of sales visits so you understand the nature of the customer, the types of sale situations and how the sales team handle them. Likewise, depending upon the business, it may also be worth joining the delivery and implementation teams at key stages of the customer satisfaction process.

I strongly recommend that having solicited the perspective of all the key parties through the steps above, and before finalising plans, you walk your way through this process step by step with the people involved. Visualise yourself as a potential customer and walk your way through each step, from initial enquiry, to being a satisfied customer making a repeat purchase.

Image: www.freepik.com - asier_relampago...

Consider which other processes are critical

It's possible that you may need to investigate the policy, process and practices in other specific areas of the business at this stage, or even earlier if the situation calls for it. These areas may include HR function and how people are recruited, retained, and developed, especially if recruiting staff is a barrier to growth for the business.

Likewise it's important to be aware of the financing and cash flow dynamics of the business, although if you have a strong finance lead, they should be on top of that.

Whether it's them explaining or you working it out, ensure you understand the drivers of cash flow and especially whether and why revenue growth generates or consumes cash.

Finally, if you have a small number of large customers, you may also need to look into legal matters such as the customer contracts and, if IP is a key asset, you may need to check out control over intellectual property rights. And of course, there may be other areas of the business that are critical and require further investigation.

Image: www.unsplash.com - arlington_research

TIPS & TRICKS

Depending on the scale of your business, the people responsible for reviewing the process with you could be individuals, teams, or team leaders.

Because of its importance I'll repeat that clearly; I strongly advise you to engage directly with the people actually doing the activities on a day to day basis. Do not rely upon the understanding of senior management.

I'm afraid what happens in reality is rarely what we senior managers believe does or should happen. And I say that, not as a criticism, but rather as a fact that I've come to realise through my own experience.

As someone who feels comfortable delving into details and processes, I've often thought that I knew everything there was to know about a particular process. Though I have learnt many times, to my cost, that I was unaware of everything that mattered at the critical, detailed level.

Month one: Week 5 Decisions

This book aims to address the needs of a generic business operating in an unknown situation. Therefore, it's important to acknowledge that I, like you, the new business leader, can't know everything about everything. Consequently in this book, I concentrate on the most critical areas that are commonly encountered by business.

And as previously suggested, as time progresses, the detail I can cover will inevitably reduce as it becomes more dependent upon the specific industry, business and situation as well as the findings from the early stages. So from now sections will be shorter and shorter, reflecting the amount of generic advice I can offer.

Develop plans

OK so now you know everything. Not! There will still be a lot you don't know, but time is of the essence. When you were appointed by stakeholders they had an expectation. When you joined, staff saw you as someone who could lead the way. They all want positive change and are looking to you for it. If you don't act soon, they'll assume that nothing will change, and it'll be harder for you to make progress. So seize the moment and take the business to the next level under your leadership.

But don't rush in quite yet. You need to be clear in your own thinking first. You only have one chance to set the agenda so if you kick off with the wrong messages and send the organisation, or at least perceptions, in the wrong direction, you will struggle to get things back on track.

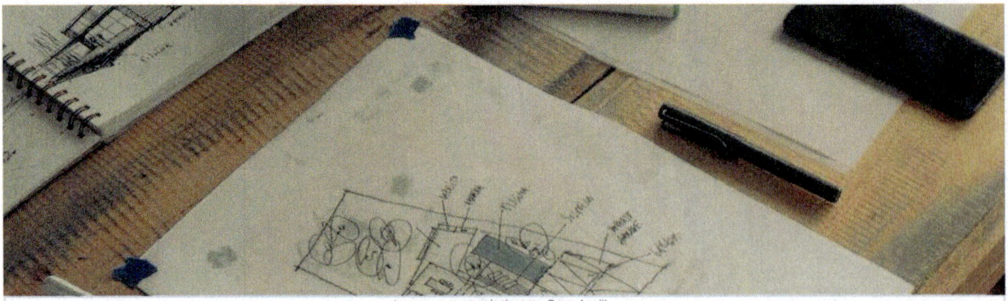

Image: www.unsplash.com - Ryan Ancill

Pause to think

Image: www.canva.com

So even though it may be challenging, take a brief moment to create some time and space for yourself to think. A month in, people will be expecting you to be in control and will be coming to you for decisions. And not just normal decisions. People are smart. They will also be trying to get you to make decisions to 'improve' things.

Note the quotes. Whilst many will be well-intentioned, the improvements they propose will be in their eyes; from their perspective. And whilst some may fit your overall plans as they emerge, others may work against you. And of course there may be a few political players trying to divert you to support their agenda or even to trip you up before you've really got started. So take care about making decisions before you are clear of your overall vision.

TIPS & TRICKS

Despite the pressure to perform and deliver results it is essential that at this point you take some time away from the business to think clearly and make good decisions.

Remember the more senior you become the less critical it is for you to **do** things yourself and more critical it becomes to make the right decisions.

Quote: *"Insist on a lot of time being spent, almost every day, to just sit and think." Warren Buffett*

Quote: *"Far too many people get weighed down in doing, and never take the time to think and feel. If you free up some time to think freely, you'll be able to see the bigger picture much easier." Richard Branson*

Let your whole brain free

I strongly recommend that during this phase you take time away from the routine. Get away from the business at least and lock yourself away as if on holiday. Put the metaphorical damp cloth over your head... And do a lot of quick thinking on the themes I'm about to mention. Oh and perhaps take some time to go for a long walk or two. Yes I'm serious. Do your thinking and write your notes and plans. And then go for a long walk. Every day. It's amazing how things clarify themselves when you stop focusing on them.

Decision A: Strategy and purpose

Strategy - Ensuring you are in the right place at the right time

This is not the place for me to explain how to define strategy. There are a vast range of techniques available and you can read the details of numerous different approaches elsewhere and in appendix E I'll share my quick summary of what I feel you need to get clear about your strategy too.

TIPS & TRICKS

As a pointer for strategy, you could google SWOT, PESTEL, Boston matrix, Porter's five forces, Blue ocean strategy, Business model canvas and Lean startup.

Purpose - A critical factor in recruitment today

It can sometimes seem to the entrepreneur somewhat esoteric to consider purpose, and maybe it is in some ways. But from experience even with a difficult turnaround where financial success is critical, I would argue there is a good reason to consider purpose. And that's simply the difficulties with recruiting and retaining staff in today's first world.

Fortunately most of us in the so-called first world are beyond pure survival mode. Most of us, and most of our staff, need income but are not desperate. And whilst many approach recruitment with a focus on income, the reality is that there are many other reasons why we get out of bed in the morning to go to work. Few people find it easy to get up for a job they hate whatever the financial incentive and need.

Image: www.canva.com

Why do people work for your business?

I would therefore countenance you to put a bit of thought into why, other than money, people work for the business. Is it because of the training and development your company offers? Is it because your company has a great reputation as an employer that will look good on their CV? What about the team and culture? Is it fun to work here? Or does your company do good in the world?

I'll elaborate a little on that last point as it feels a bit 'soft'. And it is. But look at it through the other end of the telescope. Who wants to work for a company that does bad things? Most people don't!

Business as a force for good

I have a strong view that sustainably successful businesses solve problems for their customers. Problems worth more to the customer than they charge. They make money as a result of doing so; by being good at what they do. The reason for their existence as a business doesn't start with money. That is the **result** of solving someone's problem. Perhaps that could even be called 'helping' them. A soft term but it is, I believe, the reality of good business.

So I'd challenge you at this stage to put a little time into how your business helps the world go around. How the world is a better place because of the existence of your business.

I've learnt, from taking over a business where one of my predecessors was quoted as being proudly open with staff that "We're the biggest rip-off merchants around", that it matters in recruiting, retaining and motivating great staff.

In my first 100 days I learnt that most of the staff felt ashamed to work for that company and were not all that motivated. Something I'm pleased to say I turned around by identifying and talking about how the company, when it did a good job, helped its customers improve their lives. That's not something to be ashamed about.

So looping back to the beginning of this section. For me financial success goes hand in hand with, and is indeed a consequence of, recruiting and retaining great staff and that in turn goes hand in hand with people wanting to do a good job for customers.

TIPS & TRICKS

In the book "Start With Why" Simon Sinek explores the idea that successful leaders and organisations focus on the "why" behind what they do rather than just the "what" or "how." By starting with the "why" or the purpose, cause or belief that drives a business, leaders can inspire people (both staff and customers) to take action and create a loyal following.

Image: www.freepik.com - mike.shots

Decision B: Management, structure and culture

There is a debate in the academic literature about business. Which comes first: Strategy or Culture? In my view a great academic debate of limited importance in the real world, as both are important. As a new leader, your most critical decision could be either choosing the right strategy or might be restructuring your team and its organisation.

Depending upon the situation you inherit and your judgments in your review, that may be a positive process of building the team and culture from what exists, or may involve you making some tough decisions.

The importance of role clarity

Whatever the need, defining roles and appointing people to them can be tricky. For me the fundamental challenge, if staff are to perform at their best, is role clarity.

A clear definition of who is responsible for what is important so people don't spend time conflicting and treading on each others' toes. Or arguing about whose fault it was when things go wrong because activities, responsibilities and functions are unclear or incomplete.

TIPS & TRICKS

Instead of Job descriptions use Key Result Areas (KRAs) to define the outcomes the role exists to achieve and Key Performance Indicators (KPIs), to define how success in the role is measured. See appendix F.

Manage by outcomes not activity

The traditional definition of roles is through job descriptions. That may work for you but I am not a fan of that approach. I find job descriptions tend to describe the activities of the job. They define what the role holder needs to do. And implicitly by omission what is 'not my job'.

Whilst such documents may be appropriate for very low level jobs, I feel that for most roles where we want individuals to use their initiative, they have three problems:

- What matters to a business is not what is done, but the outcome achieved.
- Defining activities rather than outcomes does not encourage the individual to find a better way to achieve the same outcome.
- Defining what to do encourages the potential for gaps in the 'It's not my job' form.

Instead, I prefer to define roles using Key Result Areas (KRAs) to define the outcomes the role exists to achieve, and Key performance Indicators (KPIs) to quantify how success in the role is measured. See appendix F for example KRAs and KPIs.

I embed those alongside more traditional job definition items such as the mandatory and desirable attributes of the person such as skills, attitudes and behaviours and accompany the set of job definitions with a RACI style role responsibility / accountability matrix.

See appendix G for an example role responsibility matrix.

Image: www.canva.com

The optimal structure

It is difficult in a general guide such as this to define any single approach to structure. Again it's a subject in its own right.

What I would acknowledge here is that rarely in the real world is it possible to achieve a perfect structure with a perfect team. And even if you do, my experience is that something will change within months to disrupt your perfect plan.

So, as with many other things as a new leader, aim for progress not perfection. Quickly put in place the best team you can achieve and then get on with delivering results. You may, probably will, need to revisit later, but you can worry about that then and restructure or re-recruit if necessary once you see the strengths and weaknesses that emerge.

In my experience, trying to plan everything in a rush, as a new leader, can become quite confusing. I have found that, especially with teams, structures and roles, there always seem to be so many interpersonal dynamics and personalities to deal with alongside what's needed by the business strategy.

Image: www.freepik.com

Begin with the end in mind - What would the perfect structure look like

So whilst my counsel generally is for progress not perfection, that doesn't mean not reaching for the stars by starting your thinking by looking at what perfection might resemble. That seems to me to be especially true when looking at organisation structures.

Start simple. Ignore the people you have and ask yourself first, what structure and roles do you really need. What would be the perfect fit for the market and strategy. Get clear on that.

Only then start to think about how the people you have available internally fit that structure, where the overlaps are and where you need to recruit externally.

Culture - What happens when you aren't in the room

Culture already exists and you will already have signalled some change

Workplace culture is being discussed a lot, but it's often misunderstood. Many companies put idealistic behaviours into carefully-crafted documents that may be shared with new hires, or posted on the wall for all employees to see. Producing such documents, especially when staff play a large part in their production may be helpful, but is rarely sufficient.

In addition, it may be that as a new CEO, and especially if you have been appointed with a mandate to change things, you may want to change the culture. In that situation asking staff to define the culture may or may not be consistent with the future strategy.

So the first consideration loops back to the reference in the section on the first week to the importance of the signals you send soon after your arrival. Very simply in most organisations people will base their behaviour on what the leader says and more importantly does. They will be watching you and paying attention to which behaviours are reinforced, punished, and ignored. So it's extremely important to think about the example you set, even in seemingly mundane everyday interactions.

Image: www.unsplash.com - Redd F

Culture as unwritten ground rules (UGRs)

Culture in any scaled-up organisation is about a lot more than the leader, and whilst most people understand its importance, working out how to get a hold of it and influence it is tricky.

Culture seems to be something ambiguous, floating above the day-to-day: difficult to grasp and challenging, although not impossible, to measure. It's one of those things that we all recognise when we see it, but which we struggle to define precisely - never mind change. Nonetheless, it is critical for the new leader to manage culture. So how can you do so?

The best approach I know is one developed and promoted by my good friend Steve Simpson, which uses a concept called UGRs or Unwritten Ground Rules. UGRs exist in every organisation on the planet. In summary, UGRs are what really makes up your company culture.

In summary, the idea is that every organisation has its rules: the written rules and the unwritten rules. The written rules (policies and procedures) are set out by the leadership and management to guide how the organisation is supposed to operate.

But note the word 'supposed.' In reality, most organisations and most people in them, are actually more powerfully guided by the informal, undefined, normally undocumented and unwritten ground rules (UGRs) of behaviour. 'The way we do things around here.' - Otherwise known as culture.

UGRs are the behaviours and routines followed by employees that complement, and importantly may contrast with and override, the official written rules, including the values statements on the wall. It is these unwritten rules that need to be managed.

For example, if a new employee begins work in the accounting department and is told that "our company encourages collaboration between departments," they might approach the purchasing department with an idea for better cross-departmental communication. If a manager tells them to stick to their own lane, they'll quickly learn that this explicit rule is not followed in practice. The UGR is actually to "not meddle".

Steve Simpson; https://www.steve-simpson.com

Is an employee judged harshly for taking time off or not working a 12-hour day? You may have a UGR that threatens work-life balance, leading to decreased employee wellbeing and causing staff turnover. Can an employee expect to be praised and/or rewarded for a job well done? Clearly it is good if you have a UGR that ensures managers show appreciation, leading to increased employee wellbeing, leading to positive company culture.

Culture as how things are done around here

UGRs are usually most visible to new joiners. They soon learn how they are supposed to operate in the organisation through looks, gestures, body language and quiet words at the coffee machine.

Image: www.unsplash.com - Austin Distel

"Didn't you know he's a Spurs fan? I'd keep out of his way when they've just lost to Arsenal." "If you want to keep your job, don't disagree with her in a meeting." "If you want to get that done by Fred, have a word with Joe. I know it's not his job, but he plays golf with Fred and if he asks Fred, it'll get done."

It is through these daily interactions that people learn "how things are done around here" and those UGRs become the reality of your workplace culture. The fact that UGRs underpin the workings of your business is not inherently bad but does mean it's important for the new leader to get a grip on them quickly, despite them being difficult to see, control, and monitor.

So how to do so? In concept the process is quite simple - by making them explicit and written! In reality it's not that simple and requires skilled, open/engaged leadership and management.

I will outline the methodology for you in the next section and depending upon the scale of your business and the resources and time you have available you can choose to follow the process yourself, or this is one of the areas where a strong, independent facilitator with expertise can help guide the process without the baggage of the internal perspective.

Managing culture and the UGRs

Essentially the methodology is to uncover, understand, agree, and most importantly live by a set of desired behaviours so that company culture aligns with a tangible and agreed set of shared values.

The three key steps, assuming you have by now a clear view of your strategy and purpose, as described earlier, are:

Awareness and take stock: Train all staff about the concept of a UGR, and what it means. Get together to talk about the common UGRs in your business. Ask them to finish the sentence, "around here...". For example, "around here, being open and honest gets you..." and understand what the UGRs currently are within your organisation.

Create positive UGRs: Discuss the UGRs openly and through workshops with staff, identify what UGRs will create the right working environment going forward. Ensuring that you, as the new leader, and your leadership team, are fully committed to them as right for enabling the future success of the organisation.

Embed positive UGRs: Incorporate these UGRs into what you do. Promote them strongly with the critical backing that anyone can challenge anyone, including you, if they feel they're not behaving in accordance with now-written ground rules. Ensure all live by the agreed written ground rules and repeat and refine as necessary.

Image: www.freepik.com - wirestock

Image: www.canva.com

The first step and last step will be the most difficult

The first is challenging as it involves encouraging honesty in getting to the core of what UGRs really exist within your organisation today.

This might involve picking apart relationships between managers and team members, and might drag up incidents or mistakes in the past. This will damage egos, but it needs to be done in order to get the existing UGRs out into the open.

The last step is equally challenging, as, for the new UGRs to become embedded, you and the leadership team have to be clearly and visibly reinforcing them.

Success at this stage depends significantly on everyone seeing you, and your leadership team, championing the new UGRs, holding people to account, and more importantly being seen to hold each other to account for following them.

Every small interaction and daily decision has a cumulative impact on the "way things are done". These UGRs are passed throughout the organisation, and given to new recruits. As the leader, you need to ensure the UGRs are positive and helpful to strategy and to future success.

TIPS & TRICKS

Your job is to enthuse and enable the team to deliver the results. Tempting as it might be, you can't do it all yourself.

Decision C: Projects, processes and systems - and project roles

Having concluded your vision, the strategy and purpose, coupled with the structure you believe is necessary to deliver results, the third area to look at is how your new vision will work and how you will get the business operating to your vision.

Build the team

The first and most important message I have for you here is that you can't do it all yourself overnight. Whilst you have to visibly take control and send signals that you know where you are leading the business and how you are going to get there, your first and most important priority is building the team. Winning hearts and minds of those you need to lead to deliver your shared grand new vision!

Notice my deliberate choice of the word lead. Your job is to enthuse and enable the team to deliver the results. Tempting as it might be, you can't do it all yourself... and you shouldn't. Your role as leader is, as my friend Lindsay Mckenna says, **"to look after the team so they look after the business."**

In this context, "looking after" the team means leading them. To have a vision of where the business is going under your leadership, to convince them that the vision is attractive for them too (hence the previous section on purpose) and to lead them consistently through the inevitably bumpy journey, overcoming the obstacles towards the goal.

Image: www.freepik.com

Whilst you need to decide (and agree with stakeholders) the overall direction; the overall strategy, structure, budget and plans, you need the team to succeed to make it happen.

You can't cover every detail. So stick to the big picture, your immediate team, a few key strategic change projects, some key capability building projects and a handful of quick win projects to drive the business forward. Then work with the team to define the detailed structures, processes, systems and people you need in place for the business to succeed in delivering the vision, and the projects you need to change the business so that it is able to achieve the vision.

Processes - The province of your management team

My second suggestion is that you do not try to define the details of the processes and systems yourself. Firstly because you probably don't know enough of the details to make the right decisions and also because 'those that plan the battle don't battle the plan'.

Being clear about the outcomes you want whilst letting the team work out how to deliver those outcomes reliably and consistently is more likely to get you the results you need.

Projects - Do less better

Your critical success factor at this point is your choice of projects and your choice of people to lead them. So choose carefully. Which are the right battles and right fronts to tackle and who are the right managers to lead each project? Are they committed to delivering the project on time and on budget?

A key tip is not to try to do too much. Better to do less successfully than to be progressing on too many fronts for any of them to be effective. So do less to achieve more. Think in terms of focusing the team around delivering 3 big (12 month) projects and 6 quick win (six week) projects. All defined by you and, as discussed under KRAs earlier, in terms of the goals or results to be achieved rather than being bogged down in the how.

Projects - Require focus, commitment and time

Which leads me to make a third recommendation. I suggest you don't assume projects 'just happen' in spare time alongside operational work. Managing change takes time and is just as valid and as important a role as ongoing line management.

A corporate manager would appoint full time professional project and programme managers. You, as an operational business leader, probably don't have the scale to justify a full-time project manager, never mind more than one. So project management in most entrepreneurial operational businesses is, I find, usually a part-time role done alongside the 'day job'.

I see that as a good thing really as it ensures the project manager properly understands the business and is committed to implementing a project that really helps the business run more efficiently and effectively.

Image: www.unsplash.com - Markus Winkler

There is however a danger that I find happens far too often. It's simply that most operational business leaders don't consciously allocate manager and staff time to delivering the change project. They implicitly expect the project to happen in the 'spare time'. Likewise performance management in most businesses is usually orientated around the line management 'day job'.

That is, I'm afraid, a recipe for project overrun. Very simply because people follow the 'what gets measured gets done' principle. If the performance management process focuses on their results as a line manager then they are unlikely to give much attention to the project however important you say it is.

To illustrate this with an example. It may be that part of the platform you envisage as enabling future success is based on implementing a modern efficient CRM system. The success of any CRM system implementation requires significant input by the sales team from director to sharp end. If their rewards and performance measures only reflect their operational sales performance, then don't be surprised if that is what takes priority and the CRM system implementation project is accorded low priority.

Image: www.freepik.com

Projects - Your key tool for performance improvement

So it is critical that you allocate a proportion of manager and team time and recognition to project delivery. Likewise, not only should you guide and monitor the performance of individuals through KRAs and KPIs as discussed earlier, some managers and some team members may also be responsible for, and rewarded for, achieving transition objectives (project goals) on time and on budget too.

Note again my focus on delegation of outcomes; of goals, not activities. Whilst clearly you need to stay close to critical strategic projects, I recommend that as far as possible you focus on delegating outcomes and use your 'clout' to help your team overcome barriers to achieving those outcomes rather than trying to delegate activities. Give your team as much freedom as you can to work out the activities needed to deliver the outcome.

Decision D: Communication and coordination

The fourth of the five key elements of your launch plan is something apparently trivial and consequently often forgotten. How does the organisation communicate?

Image: www.canva.com

In my experience this is a critical decision for the operational business leader. In many organisations meetings happen by accident without a lot of planning. As a result things happen without the right people being aware and involved. And by contrast other matters get held up as unnecessary and in reality (although they would never admit it) irrelevant people join the debate slowing down progress and decision making and diluting accountability.

Instead I believe that you, as the new business leader, should explicitly consider communication and design communication processes in conjunction with structure. The goal being to ensure clarity over decision-making processes and accountability and ideally, to involve all the appropriate individuals while excluding those who do not need to be part of that specific decision.

Communication processes: Meetings with purpose

My key tip in designing the communication processes is to be very clear over the purpose of each meeting. Is it a one-way meeting for information sharing? Is it a meeting to discuss something and develop ideas so that an accountable manager can go away to plan implementation? Is it a consultation where a manager or director presents a proposal and asks for feedback so they are fully informed to make the best possible decision?

It is difficult to propose a correct decision-making process for all businesses with much of the detail depending upon the nature of the business and its specific trading cycle. There is a big difference between a business that sells 2000 items a day through an eCommerce site and one that wins one massive tender each year.

However, it is possible for me to recommend organising meetings and communication processes based on a regular cycle of daily, weekly, monthly, and annual intervals. So on this topic I'll illustrate using an example of what meetings might happen in your hypothetical business.

Image: www.unsplash.com - wocintechchat

Daily

9am. Each department has a 'standup'. The dozen members of each team get together for 15 mins and discuss with their team leader the priorities for the day. The team highlights barriers to success and asks for help, management support and direction on critical matters and blockers to success.

5pm. Your senior management team gets together to review the successes of the day and consider the priorities for the next day. Each senior manager shares the top three success stories of that day, the things they want to get accomplished the next and most importantly, the things they think might detract from the success.

Weekly

Tuesday is your company office day. All staff are expected to work in the office that day. At 10am all 30 team leaders attend a KPI meeting. At that meeting each shares, in less than 1 minute on screen, last week's outcome vs budget for up to three KPIs for their department. As the cost of 30 people in the meeting is high, this is a one way communication meeting. There is no discussion of the KPIs at the meeting. Instead individual directors and managers are encouraged to meet up with each other later in the day to address issues arising.

During the day, managers and team leaders are expected to have one-on-one conversations with each individual who reports to them. This is done to gain insight into the individual's work and personal life, and to determine how the manager can assist them in achieving their business, project, and personal goals.

Monthly

Board Meeting

Your key business meeting each month is the board meeting. The purpose of the board meeting in this example is to ensure business continuity, review historic performance, look forward at trends and consider what actions might be needed across the business (without taking away the authority of individual directors to decide and be accountable for their own area).

Most importantly however, is to make business critical decisions that could have a major impact on the survival of the business, or which impact more than one directorate and where the respective directors have been unable to agree a way forward. I provide a brief summary of how I feel board meetings should work in appendix H and how they should be minuted in appendix I.

Image: www.freepik.com - rawpixel

Image: www.freepik.com - prostooleh

Project progress review meetings

In all the businesses I have run, there have consistently been cross-company projects. A useful meeting format was therefore a monthly project review, in which the project manager presents an update on the progress of their project using both the standard four-box report and conventional project management documents.

Typically, these meetings are chaired by the project sponsor and involve a broader audience including most of the individuals involved in the project and often all or most of the directors whose departments are participating in the project. As such they would be more detailed than the overview presented to the board.

CEO Breakfast / Lunch

I personally found it useful to have an informal meeting each month with all new joiners, inviting a representative from every department to attend, deliberately mixing grades of staff from first level through to director.

A good exercise is to ask all the existing staff members to introduce themselves with the most senior people going first. I'd ask them to share one thing that they love about the company and one thing that is bugging them about their job at the moment. And then I'd give the new joiners the chance to say hello and, depending upon their seniority, ask them to talk about their background and why they have joined the company.

Quarterly

A key meeting for the businesses I have run was the quarterly strategic review. This fairly large meeting would take place offsite once a quarter and end with an informal dinner. The precise structure of the meeting would vary depending on where we were in the year, but in general the format would be a workshop reviewing progress against our strategic objectives and/or discussing what was important going forward. Note that this was always a workshop to debate and discuss, not make decisions. My strong belief is that team leaders, managers, and directors should be the ones consulting to understand and gain support and then deciding, rather than committees. The board should be responsible for making the most significant decisions, after conducting thorough analysis, careful consideration, and debate.

Image: www.freepik.com - rawpixel

Annual

The key event in the calendar each year for me would be the annual company conference where all staff spend a day out of the office participating in professionally run workshops designed to engage staff members across the business with other people from different departments and to help everyone understand the business, strategy and plans going forward.

Christmas and summer social

Strangely, but actually understandably, the events that most businesses plan in detail are the Christmas or Summer social. So with that, and also recognising the variation in feasibility for different businesses, I won't comment much other than recommending that every business has a Christmas social and if practical a summer family barbecue. Using social events to build relationships between people, alongside thanking the family of staff, is generally helpful in building loyalty.

By the way, as December gets busy, especially for those with families, I've found it fairly popular to hold the Christmas social in mid January to blow away the dark night blues.

Decision E: Budget and financial plan

As most readers will be familiar with the processes of financial reporting and budget setting I will only cover this briefly with the comment that they are critical but difficult, especially for a new leader.

Expectations of you as the wonderful new leader will be high so there will be pressure to be ambitious, but at the same time I would highlight that knowledge is limited, so be cautious. Sadly this is an area where only experience in dealing with people, especially stakeholders, can help you to judge the appropriate balanced way forward.

Imbalanced impact of balanced decisions

I'd just share one tip, based on my mistakes over the years. My model used to be that recognising the chances of getting budgets and plans exactly right is near to zero, they should be put forward with a 50% chance of over achieving and a 50% chance of under achieving.

I now recognise that was a flawed approach for the simple reason that the consequences of an under achievement, especially in a self-funded small business can be much more material than an over achievement.

Image: www.unsplash.com - Rifath (Photoripey)

Think cashflow. The impact of having £100k more cash at year end than planned is positive but limited in consequence. The impact of having £100k less cash might be catastrophic as it might make the business insolvent or at least outside bank covenants.

In those circumstances I would want a budget that we had an 80% or even greater chance of achieving. And the consequence of that would be to have both a conservative budget (which we MUST achieve or exceed) and a target that is a stretch but we believe we can achieve.

Month one: Week 6
Finalise plans, communicate and launch

Finalise Plans

Okay, I'm adding an extra week or two on to your first month, but you get the picture. In fact this period will fly by so quickly it'll certainly still feel like the first month. Also it's worth reiterating that these timings are generic and therefore approximate.

The time frame that it takes to make decisions, develop and thus finalise plans will obviously be specific to you, your business and its unique situation. But once you've seen enough to finalise your plans it's time to communicate and launch them.

Action 5: Ensure support

This is a small step but an important one. One I missed, or at least did minimally, to my cost. Having drafted your plans, test them with key advisors and most importantly your stakeholders. The people that appointed you and potentially others such as your bank manager and key business partners. That might include customers and suppliers but be careful not to offer them the ability to determine your business strategy.

Image: www.unsplash.com - Towfiqu Barbhuiyt

Action 6: Plan the launch sequence - especially the difficult stuff

The final step of the last preliminary phase is to plan the launch, along with outlining the process and sequence of communication. Note that sequence is very important.

Image: www.unsplash.com - Ivan Diaz

Ensure timely communication

Again I learnt, this time earlier in my career from my boss's mistake, how important it is to communicate with all relevant parties very quickly, efficiently and effectively. It's amazing how fast the grapevine works when there is significant news. Two problems I had to deal with as a result of my boss's omission were with sales people and with customers.

The restructuring was announced formally to the stock market at 9 am. Within minutes the phone lines were going crazy with customers asking what the impact would be on their account and their contract / trade. As Operations director at that time, customer service was my problem and I quickly had to develop a 'line' (a consistent and accurate but non-detailed message) for our staff to use to quell the concerns and reassure customers.

The impact of not spelling out the detail of the plans through the sales force was slightly more delayed. It emerged a week or two later when I (because I had good relationships with the key staff at our major customers) started to get calls saying; "Please can you get your act together and call off your sales team! I have had numerous calls from different sales staff claiming that they are now handling everything for our account".

It transpired that the changes to the sales force had not been worked through in detail so there was ambiguity over who was handling which account and sales people being sales people, were entrepreneurially trying to claim ownership of existing accounts themselves.

Completely rational. A much easier way to gain a revenue stream than winning a new account! But not helpful to the business and our credibility overall with the client!

The difficult stuff

Managing the impact of change on people is one of the trickiest elements of any restructuring, whether it's due to a new leader or any other reason. Obviously that is particularly the case if there is potential for roles to be made redundant.

You should keep in mind that there are many angles to managing restructuring, and the full detail of this topic would require a book in itself. However, I can offer you a few brief tips to help you navigate this process.

Image: www.unsplash.com - LinkedIn

Why am I doing this?

Firstly, I suggest you clear your mind by posing the question to yourself, "Do I genuinely believe that the restructuring I am leading is in the best interests of the business and sustaining (or re-establishing) its success in the future?" If that isn't the case then you need to look in the mirror and ask yourself why are you doing it? Assuming, as you should be able to, that you are doing the right thing, then the rest follows from that solid foundation.

By following that plan, you make sure that the company's future is secure, consequently protecting the interests of all stakeholders, including the workforce. If you have the sad, onerous and emotionally painful responsibility of making redundancies, you need to be comfortable about why you have to do so.

If the foundation of doing it for the right reasons is in place then be clear you are doing it, not because you want to cause people a painful experience, but because you have a duty to protect the futures of those remaining.

That might be easier to understand in reverse. What would be the consequences of you failing in your duty and ducking the tough decisions and emotionally difficult process? Presumably it would be a less successful business at higher risk of losing the support of its backers, and with your successor likely to have to make even more redundancies and potentially even the business closing down and everyone losing their jobs.

The same rationale applies to tough decisions being communicated to your customers and suppliers albeit usually, but not always, with a lower level of emotion attached.

Image: www.freepik.com - rawpixel

Your responsibility is to be respected not liked or agreed with

My final comment on managing the difficult stuff is that your goal should not be that those affected understand and accept your (the) decision as correct. That is generally difficult to achieve. Why would anyone accept their role should be one that is no longer needed?

Instead my counsel is that your objective should be that those employees say "I don't agree with their decision, but I have to say my boss behaved very professionally and fairly in the way they implemented it". Two years later, once they have regained stability, they may also admit they can see why it was the right decision, but that's a bonus that's only happened to me twice. Indeed in one case they approached me for a role with a new business I'd later joined. So it can happen. But don't count on it!

Image: www.freepik.com - Drazen Zigic

Action 7: Launch

For continuing staff

How you deliver the message is obviously situation dependent. It may or may not be possible or even desirable to have all staff in the same place at the same time. And if you have difficult messages to convey to just some of the staff, you may need to meet them separately and probably first.

Be open and straightforward

Which immediately relates to your first key messages. Don't try to hide them or avoid them or cover them up. Be clear, concise and positive. Which means you have to get them absolutely clear in your own head first.

Acknowledge the pain

A first key message for the majority of the staff is likely to be to acknowledge that change isn't always easy and may be painful for some. Maybe something like "I know this change will be difficult for some and disruptive for us all. It's something we need to do in order to achieve... (this bright future)... for the business, for all of us in it and for our customers, suppliers, shareholders and other stakeholders".

My view is that if you have had to make some tough decisions for others (who are probably friends with some of those remaining) it is wise to acknowledge that openly and be positive about them (redundancy of a role is a consequence of a business situation, not a comment on them personally) and explain at a high level why the decision is necessary.

Image: www.unsplash.com - Jakob Dalbjorn

Share the strategy and purpose positively and clearly

Moving back to the key messages. This is your first and most critical opportunity to communicate the strategy and purpose of the business in one or two clear simple statements. That is critical.

You need your team to understand that you have a clear vision, and the business has a clear positive purpose and position. Whether they realise it or not, they are looking for you to convey the feeling that you have a clear direction and are going to take the business to a better place. They need to understand their role in the world through understanding the role of the business in the world. To quote Simon Sinek again, "It starts with why". (A great book by the way)

You may also want to go on to set out some of the details of the key changes coming, key projects and quick wins. Or you may not. That is situation dependent. All I'd highlight is that this (re)launch meeting is a great chance for you to set the scene for the next few months and maybe even the next few years.

Unite the team behind messages that will stand the test of time

I remember one of my messages in one new role was "I want us to lead this industry in behaviour if not in scale... yet". There was a lot behind that carefully crafted message. Positively I wanted us to be innovative in driving changes in the way the industry worked.

And there was a negative behaviour I wanted to address too. People were getting cross when competitors copied our good initiatives. My intention was to shift the emotion from one of anger and frustration to that of pride. "Imitation is the greatest form of flattery". The "yet" at the end was to imply that leading in behaviour and causing everyone else to run around copying us would ultimately lead to us leading in scale too.

Image: www.canva.com

Create a sense of urgency

Finally, even though, as explained before, this book aims to provide a comprehensive overview for different types of businesses, industries, and sizes and so is inevitably general, it is important to note that there is one more message that almost every new leader should impart. Urgency!

I have never come across a situation where senior management and external stakeholders were not asking the new leader to deliver results quickly. It goes with the territory! So use your launch meeting to create **urgency**.

The typical technique for that is creating the perception of being on a "burning platform". ie 'Something bad will happen' if action isn't taken quickly. As always the precise details of that will depend upon your business.

All I know is that if you want change to happen, you as the leader have to create that sense of urgency amongst the staff. If they don't feel they are on borrowed time, they will resist change until another day "when they have more time".

For staff that may be leaving

Finally let me turn to your communication with the others; those impacted in a potentially painful way by the decisions.

Be open and accepting of their right to be angry with you

Communicating to them separately allows you to tailor the message to their situation. I've found it best to acknowledge openly that you realise the decision isn't one that they will welcome and they may be cross with you and that's OK and understandable.

Your position is that you have not avoided making the decision, as you have a responsibility to act in the best interests of the company without fear or favour. You will however ensure that it is implemented fairly, professionally and with respect and support for them as individuals.

Be positive with them as individuals

Talking about the bright future for the business is unlikely to be the appropriate message to convey to them. However a positive message that can inspire hope for their future is still generally desirable.

Sometimes the reality is that people who are in a role that isn't working are unhappy but don't feel confident in resigning and finding a new job. By making the decision for them, you are opening up the opportunity for them to pursue a more fulfilling role.

Clearly though that doesn't apply to all and it's difficult to say that directly without appearing patronising. But if you can find a way to focus them on the potential for a positive future for them, that is an encouraging message to convey.

Final comments on the launch

I have assumed the need for a big launch meeting, or series of meetings - an 'all hands' meeting' - or to use modern parlance a 'town hall'. I have always judged that to be the case and believe it will nearly always be the case.

I guess if you were recruited to maintain the status quo and the strategy is steady as she goes with minimal change then maybe that's an exception, although even then I think staff will want to hear from you. So you'll probably want to meet them and reassure them that nothing is changing somehow.

Image: www.freepik.com

Take care of yourself

And finally, don't forget to look after yourself. Taking on a new role always has a degree of stress. Taking on a new leadership role multiplies that stress as you're dealing with change for everyone you lead as well as yourself.

You may be working many long hours. Question whether that is necessary and whatever you do make sure you have a means of coping with the pressure. If you go to the gym, keep it up. If you go for walks, keep doing them. If you have a coach, meet them regularly. If you are a member of a business leader peer group like MD2MD, don't skip the meetings however busy you feel you are.

Remember the business needs you to be on top form more than ever during the next few months so it is not unreasonable for the business to support you with time and money to perform at your best.

First quarter: Weeks 7-14
Make an impact

As set out at the beginning, this book can only provide general guidelines and as time goes on, challenges become increasingly tailored to the specific needs of your business. Therefore, the last section of this book can only offer a brief, clichéd approach as it simply involves implementing the plans discussed earlier in the book.
So for the sake of completeness, here is my guidance.

Build credibility by delivering quick wins - and celebrating them

Deliver the quick wins fast so you have the credibility to drive through the bigger and longer projects.

Ensure you kick off and deliver the major projects while you are new and listened to. Momentum seems important. If once you are well embedded you are seen as someone who will let deadlines and targets be missed then you will find it impossible to regain the momentum... ever.

As part of conveying momentum, good practice is to communicate your progress and goals achieved weekly with credits and positive reinforcement to those doing the great work of delivering change.

Fine tune as you learn

And finally don't be afraid to change course a little as you learn more about the best way to achieve the goal. Note that the goal, if identified carefully, is unlikely to change. It is the activities necessary to achieve the goal that tend to change.

Image: www.unsplash.com - Sebastian Pociecha

However much work you put in, you can't know everything in your planning phase and get everything right. So get going, be clear on the goal, head in roughly the right direction and then quickly adjust what you do. I love the phrase **"Ready, fire, aim"**. That conveys the idea that the goal and target remain constant, but our initial direction was a little off and we need to adjust our actions slightly.

Progress not perfection

Some might challenge the previous paragraph by pointing out the need to get things right first time, every time. I also agree with that goal.

For me there is a subtle element that is often missed. "Right" does not always mean perfect. To a customer "right" includes the dimensions of "When I need it" and "At a price I can afford". So to spend too long producing a product after the customer has gone elsewhere or that is too perfect and therefore too expensive is not "Right" for the (ex) customer.

Make haste slowly

It's a critical measure of the judgement of a leader to get the right balance as the same applies the other way. Another phrase I feel I've had to learn too often is to "Make haste slowly" or "To go faster, go slower". Slightly nonsensical phrases at face value but perhaps in reality meaningful as they reflect the conflicts a good leader has to reconcile to achieve optimum results. To deliver products or services that operate to the level of performance needed at the time needed, within the budget needed, by their chosen market.

Review and learn

The final step, towards the end of the first 100 days should, I feel, be to review progress with your management team. Perhaps you could call a strategic review 'away day'.

However you do it, it is important to identify, highlight, celebrate and promote things that have gone well and to learn from what hasn't. And conclusions on both fronts might lead you, and hopefully now your engaged management team, to identify some improvements to the longer term strategy, plans, projects and priorities... because no one gets it all right, first time!

And anyway you now need to be moving into normal management mode where your team is gradually taking the lead on many matters within your overall brief.

Image: www.unsplash.com - Unseen Studio

First year
Deliver sustainable profitable growth

I have little to add in this final section because everything I could say would be about good leadership and management in general, rather than about the specifics of being a newly appointed leader.

Change is normal

Your projects and the associated reviews should become part of your normal routine. I don't believe businesses ever get to steady state; to perfection. Your budgeting will probably migrate to an annual planning cycle with quarterly progress reviews and re-forecasts. And life for you becomes normal as the established leader.

Make yourself redundant

Indeed I would go further and share that one of my mantras as a leader was that my job was always to make myself redundant, by putting in place people and processes that delivered consistently, so that I was free to do other things.

Image: www.freepik.com - rawpixel

Because you should never be

And the thing is, there are always other things. If, perchance, you've managed to get your ducks in a line and everything is operating reasonably well within the business, then as a great operational business leader you now have another job.

You need to be outside the business looking for opportunities to use that platform of success to do more, better.

To grow the business, serve more customers, solve even more of the challenges of the world, make it a better place and by doing so earn a decent living for yourselves and your backers.

Image: www.freepik.com -DilokaStudio

Appendices
A-J

Appendix A
Tips for meeting staff

My favourite questions for staff

- ✓ What's really good about this organisation? Where are its real strengths?
- ✓ What do we need to be better at?
- ✓ And if you were sitting in my chair what would your top three first priorities be?

Tips for meeting staff

As a new business leader, your first meeting with staff is a critical opportunity to make a good first impression and start building trust. Here are a few tips for how to make the most of this meeting...

Image: www.freepik.com

Come prepared. Do enough research before you meet with them that you can ask wise questions, but don't feel you have to know everything.

Introduce yourself and your role and set expectations carefully. Give a brief overview of your background and personality, and explain your goal is to take the business forward in the best way you can. Explain that you need their help to get a better understanding of the business, how it works and their view of its strengths and weaknesses. Explain too that you are information gathering and will not be making decisions at this stage.

Ask questions and win hearts and minds by listening actively. Use the meeting to start to build a strong relationship. As the discussion progresses show you are also interested in them and their personal goals and drivers. Ask questions about their goals and their challenges too. When they are talking, really listen to what they have to say. Ask questions to clarify what they mean, and show interest and your genuine desire to build rapport.

Avoid the traps. Keep to the common theme, don't jump to decisions and actions too early. Smart members of staff might try to get you to support something that matters to them before you know enough to decide. If asked to share a view about something, explain that your knowledge is limited, you don't have any magic solutions. At this stage you are simply eager to learn about them and their work and will announce your plans, after taking into account their input and that of others, in due course. Likewise don't express opinions on people, past or present. Be especially neutral about your predecessor. You don't know what residual relationships and loyalties may exist.

Be yourself and be positive. Project an air of confidence and optimism. Although you are there to ask questions, you are in control and will lead the organisation well. Don't try to be someone you're not. The team will be able to tell if you're being fake, and it will only make it harder to build trust. Thank them for their time, let them know that you are looking forward to working with them and reaffirm that plans will be revealed later down the road.

Appendix B
Tips for meeting customers

My favourite questions for customers

- Why do you buy from us? What do you like most about our products or services?
- What was our best service moment? Who provides the best answers to your questions during the sales process?
- Can you tell me about the last time you had a difficult interaction with us and what it took for us to get it right?
- Is there anything that we could do better in terms of support after the sale? What could we improve overall?
- What are your criteria for choosing a supplier? What is most important to you? Quality, price, delivery time, customer service, or something else?
- How do we compare to other suppliers you've worked with? What would make us stand out from the competition?
- What are your biggest challenges? How can we help you overcome those challenges?
- What do we need to do to develop and extend our relationship further? What could we do to earn more of your business? What would make you more likely to do business with us in the future? What would make you more likely to choose us over our competitors?

Top tips for conducting customer interviews

Be prepared. Do your research on the customer's industry and business before you meet with them. This will help you to ask informed questions and get a better understanding of their needs.

Be open and honest. Let the customer know that you are new and that you are eager to learn about them and their business. Be open to feedback but also be clear that because you are new you don't yet know the detailed operation of the business, so can't necessarily resolve things instantly. Your commitment to them is to listen, to note and ensure things are addressed and most importantly to ensure your business is a great supplier to them on an ongoing basis.

Listen actively. When the customer is talking, really listen to what they have to say. Don't just wait for your turn to talk. Ask questions to clarify what they mean, and show that you are interested.

Be positive and upbeat but be yourself and honest. Project an air of confidence and optimism. This will help to create a positive atmosphere and make the customer feel more comfortable with you. Don't try to be someone you're not and don't promise what you don't know for sure that you can deliver. Same as your staff, the customer will be able to tell if you're being fake and if you make a promise that your business is later unable to fulfil you'll simply be creating bigger problems for yourself later.

Image: www.unsplash.com - charlesdeluvio

Appendix C
Tips for meeting suppliers

My favourite questions for suppliers

- What are your strengths as a supplier?
- How do you see our business? What do you like about working with us?
- What can we do better? How can we make it easier for you to supply us with better products and services more efficiently, more cheaply and more reliably?
- How can you help us develop our business? What else do we need to do to develop and extend our relationship further?

Image: www.freepik.com

Tips for conducting supplier meetings

Do your homework before you meet. Take the time in advance to learn about their company, their positioning, their history in the industry and with your business. This will add credibility to the relationship and enable you to appreciate their areas of strength.

Gauge their perception of your business and the relationship between you. Ask questions to understand what's working well and uncover pain points that may need to be addressed. How important is your business to them? Do they view your company as a significant customer, or just another client in their portfolio? Understanding this will give you an idea of how much leverage you have in negotiating better prices or improving service levels.

Assess the state of the relationship. How well does your business work with them at the moment? Is there a clear and transparent relationship and a mutual understanding of how you help each other succeed? Suppliers have a unique perspective on your business, and they may notice things that you or your team have overlooked.

Image: www.freepik.com - Drazen Zigic

Appendix D
Tips for meeting stakeholders

My favourite questions for an investor or banker

- ✓ What are your reasons for investing in this business?
- ✓ What are your priorities as an investor? How do you balance risk, growth and profit?
- ✓ What do we need to do to keep you supportive as an investor?

Image: www.canva.com

Appendix E
Four key elements of strategy

Strategy

Four key elements of strategy to get clear

1. **Define your market very precisely.** Make sure you are very clear on the characteristics that define your customer and, if B2B, the role and persona / personality of the key buyer within the customer business.

2. **Make sure you are clear on how your business creates value for your customer.** Ensure you know how your business is seen to add value by your customer. Where 'customer' includes both the company and the individual(s) doing the buying. Is their purchase driven by moving away from pain or towards a gain? Is it fear or greed? And why do they buy now rather than delay? What would they lose by deferring the purchase?

3. **Understand your business model.** What is your channel to market that allows you to reach them efficiently? Who are your key suppliers and what is your supply chain? What is your core process and business model that allows you to reach them and serve customers profitably?

4. **What is your competitive position?** Precisely why do customers buy from you specifically? What is different between you and your competitors? What is your 'unfair' competitive advantage? Something you have the ability to do or offer that they don't? What are the "barriers to entry" that stop new entrants undermining your business? What stops them copying you and your business model?

Appendix F
KRAs : Key result areas and KPIs

One of the challenges many business leaders will be familiar with is the refrain "it's not my job", or more likely "it wasn't my job". And very often with fast growing, innovative, and therefore evolving businesses when jobs are defined using traditional job descriptions that define a role as a set of tasks or activities or responsibilities, it isn't.

The model I came across many years ago and have adapted and refined in my roles as a business leader uses a slightly different approach that is much more useful, especially when an organisation is growing and changing rapidly.

It's simply to define roles not by what is done, but as a set of key result areas to be achieved, leaving room for the capable intelligent human to work out how best to deliver that outcome in the circumstances they find themselves.

There are two key differences:

- The outcomes required tend to change less rapidly as the world and the organisation grows and evolves
- This approach treats the team as intelligent individuals and gives them the flexibility to innovate and find better ways to do things and not to feel constrained by how it's always been done

Going further I have, over the years, realised that many key result areas apply to many businesses. For example, most businesses need to "Discuss qualified opportunities with qualified prospects through to them making a decision to procure from us". The differences are mainly in how the activities are done. As a result I have developed a base template of some typical key result areas that apply to many businesses.

I can also provide a copy of this template to anyone interested. Simply message me on LinkedIn to ask for a copy.

Appendix G
Role / Responsibility matrix

One of the challenges I have found leading small and even larger medium sized businesses is gaining and retaining clarity over who does what. It seems to be an especially problematic challenge when the business is innovative and fast growing. A goal we business leaders usually drive - with vigour. Consequently the business may have evolved in a way that is more speedily pragmatic than logical.

That is often especially visible to the new CEO. Very often the new CEO is the person who sees the anomalies and inconsistencies. Roles that were probably not that clearly defined in the first place have since evolved and responsibilities - and more critically accountability - have become muddled.

Not only that, but the fast growth of an organisation often means the nature of someone's involvement in a role or a project may not ever have been clear in the first place.

Image: www.canva.com

I completely understand why this happens. I may even have been guilty myself! I can hear myself now asking "Ben, would you mind helping Project Skylark for a few hours each week please?" If Skylark (perhaps the development and launch of a new product) is successful, a year later that comment could easily have led to Skylark being the largest part of Ben's job"

So you, as a new business leader, face two challenges in your first 100 days. Firstly in the early days you need to understand who does what, and later once you've decided how you want to take the business forward, you need to communicate who you want to do what in any new structure you choose to implement.

Most people are familiar with the organisation chart and that can be helpful as a picture of who reports to who. But an organisation chart doesn't usually help you understand who does what in the various processes and systems.

Such detail is usually buried in tedious job descriptions which no one reads (unless there is a problem) and are rarely kept up to date. I have suggested how job descriptions can be improved through the use of KRAs but even then it is often difficult to see how job roles interact without reading through a number of different documents.

Image: www.unplash.com - Alex Kotliarskyi

My solution is a tool, evolved from the RACI matrix often used in project management. (Please Google for details of RACI if you're interested - I've tried not to digress into too many project management tools in this book).

I call the tool a role / responsibility matrix and I maintain it as spreadsheet. I believe this tool has some important benefits:

- ✓ It is compact - It can be kept to one page
- ✓ You can see who is involved in activities, their role in the activity and the relationship between their role and that of others.
- ✓ It clearly distinguishes between who does, who decides, who is consulted and who is informed. This is, in my experience, very muddled in many organisations.
    - People who are consulted often feel that implies they have a decision making role. Later, when the decision, based on numerous inputs, is different to what they wanted it becomes "You didn't listen to what I said".
    - Distinguishing between consulted and decides helps understanding so that "We did listen but the conclusion we reached after consulting numerous people was a different one" becomes slightly more acceptable.
    - Similar comments apply to the distinction between execution (doing) and decision making. I have known far too many business leaders and marketing managers pulling their hair out at the words that have been published on the website by the IT or even marketing department.

Find an example of a simplified role responsibility matrix on the next page.

Example
Role / Responsibility matrix

An example role responsibility matrix for a small consultancy

	Owner	Finance	Operations	Consultants	Marketing	Customers	Web supplier	Other suppliers
Strategy	XD	c	c	c	c	c		
Writing case studies	xD	i	i	d	X	c		
Drafting and issuing press releases	xD	i	i	i	X	i	i	
Drafting words for brochures and web	xD			i	X		i	x
Developing content for website	xD	i	i	i	x	c	X	c
Writing and sending interesting newsletters	xd		i	i	Xd	cl	x	c
SEO and getting backlinks for Website	xD						Xd	
Updating website	xD	X	c	i	i	i	Xd	
Participating in blogs and forums	xD			d	d	d		d
Managing contacts database	xd	x	x	x	XD	c		
Planning / arranging meeting dates & venues	xC		X	c	c	c		
Booking meeting with right equipment	c		X	cd		c		C
Liaison with client pre & post meeting	c		Xd	x		C		
Planning and organising client meetings	c		X	cd		c		c
Preparing for meetings	D		x	X				
Facilitate client meeting	XD			X		x		C
Soliciting and analysing feedback	i	i	XD	i	i	c		
Getting contract details documented for new projects	xD	C	x	X		xD		
Invoicing customers	d	x	X	x		i		
Getting invoices paid	d	X	x	x		i		
Paying supplier bills	d	X	x					i

X = eXecute (Do it!)
D = Decide
C= Consulted
I = informed

x = eXecute some
d = participate in decision
c= may be consulted
i = may be informed

Appendix H
Properly focused board meetings

Board meeting
Principles

I like board meetings to be relatively short (say 2 hours) and very tightly focused on formally reviewing the state of the company, so all directors have a shared understanding. Then making 'big bet' decisions for the company based on a clear written proposal circulated in advance setting out the options and the pros and cons of each.

In my view everyone should be aware of the topic and the issues in advance so they can consider their view properly, identify for themselves the key influences and be able to decide their view, based on proper consideration and probably consultation.

Likewise I believe informal discussions in advance of the board meeting, maybe with non-board participants, are the appropriate way to explore options and gain clarity over the decision, the options and the pros and cons.

I see the board meeting itself as the tip of the iceberg where the options and their pros and cons are set out clearly in a report to the board, so that the board can quickly assess them against each other and decide which to follow, if necessary by voting to ascertain where the weight of opinion sits.

Image: www.freepik.com - rawpixel

TIPS & TRICKS

My view is that the role of the board is only to make decisions that either have a material impact across more than one part of the business or decisions that could determine overall the success or failure of the business.

I do not believe that the board should make decisions that only impact within the responsibility of one director. For example appointing a member of their staff. They should make those decisions, probably after consulting their co-directors, and be accountable for the decision and delivering the result.

That approach should also, in my view, be cascaded down. Decisions should be taken at the lowest possible level and the person making the decision being supported to make the right decision and held accountable, albeit with acceptance that none of us is perfect, for the results.

Board meeting

Agenda

1. Review the past by looking at historic KPIs and financial results vs budget
2. Consider the future by looking at forecast financial performance based on an extrapolation from the KPI trends adjusted for known events and changes
    a. My personal preference is for a rolling 13 month forecast showing the month just ended through to the same month next year
3. Review risks to business continuity, reviewing compliance reports and business risk register
4. Receive a presentation from each director on their area of responsibility based on a one page four box report. You'll see an example of one in appendix J.
5. Receive a similar presentation from the project manager of each key business change project
6. To make business critical decisions (**See below) based on brief evidenced papers setting out the situation, the alternative options, the pros and cons of each and the recommended decision of the director responsible

Appendix I
Board minutes - how and why they matter

Most business leaders know that minutes are a summary of what happened at a company board meeting. That much is straightforward and most directors understand the principles of HOW to write minutes but I find many misunderstand the underlying principles of WHY well-written board minutes are important to you as a director.

I've been a director for a quarter of a century but I think it was only about ten years ago I really understood the full purpose of minutes and I regularly see minutes today that miss key aspects, which reflects a failure to understand why we produce minutes.

By the way, I also know many businesses don't really have board meetings or minutes. That is a big mistake for the directors involved and I hope in this appendix to cover why well-constructed board minutes matter and why not producing them is dangerous.

Before reading, please note a caution; whilst I am an experienced director with reasonable governance experience, I am not a lawyer so do use your own due diligence and consult your own lawyer for full precise legal guidance.

Image: www.unsplash.com - Unseen studio

How to write minutes

Let's begin with the relatively well-understood basics of HOW to write minutes.

Minutes are a written record of what happened at a meeting. They help the board to make decisions and can be used as a reference point in the future. So writing minutes is an important responsibility for the business, as it helps to ensure that the board functions effectively and transparently.

The minutes of a board meeting should be a fair and accurate record of what was discussed and agreed upon. They should not be a verbatim account but should instead capture the key points.

Image: www.canva.com

Minutes should be unbiased and objective. They should also be accurate, concise and readable so that anyone who reads them can easily understand the key elements of the discussion as well as the decisions and actions agreed by the directors.

The following guidelines will help you get the basics right:

1. Stick to the facts. Minutes should be an objective summary of the discussions that took place, without embellishment or opinion.
2. Be thorough. Minutes should record all important elements of the discussion, the actions agreed and the decisions made.
3. Be consistent. Minutes should be formatted in a consistent way so that they are easy to read and understand.

Image: www.canva.com

Why we write minutes

Now let's turn to the more important, but the less well understood, matter of WHY we write minutes. A critical angle as it influences how they are written. It also explains what distinguishes minutes that are good and useful for the business and the directors from those that are less so.

Business board minutes are written for three main reasons and each reason leads us to consider a different element of the content. These reasons are listed opposite and the following paragraphs provide a little more detail on each.

1. To record carefully the precise decisions of the board
2. To capture commitments made by individual directors to the board
3. To record at a high level the matters discussed and, most importantly, the rationale behind decisions.

Decisions

This is the most commonly understood reason for minutes. What is sometimes missed is the need for precision as to what is decided. It is not at all uncommon for different parties to a decision to leave a discussion with different understandings of what was agreed.

Decisions should therefore be based on a clearly worded resolution, possibly around a pre-prepared board paper.

For example a decision 'to progress the development of the new Hyperdynamic product' means very little without supporting detail within the resolution or a separate (and carefully filed) board paper setting out the business benefits and risks of the investment.

At the very least it should read "The board agreed to invest £100,000 and deploy Joe full-time to develop the Hyperdynamic product with the goal of market launch on 1st January and first customers on board by 31st March".

Image: www.freepik.com - Snowing

Commitments and actions

This isn't really a matter limited to board records. Recording commitments in board minutes is simply good management practice in capturing the accountability of directors to the board.

It is therefore more a part of the management process and, if it ever becomes necessary, a director performance management process. As such it is more akin to any other management accountability process at all levels throughout an organisation.

Discussion and rationale

This is the area many, including me in my early career as a director, miss. It is not good enough for minutes to simply capture what decision was made for the business.

The minutes also need to capture the discussion leading to the decision, including why the board made that decision. More precisely they need to show that the board was appropriately diligent and thorough in making the decision.

And although often missed, this is in fact probably the most important purpose of the minutes. To show that the board were suitably thorough in assessing the considerations involved when making an important decision on behalf of the business. Or, to turn it around, were not negligent in making the decision.

Which immediately leads to why this is the case. The time that board minutes become of real vital importance, and why every company board should keep thorough records, is when something goes wrong.

When there is an attempt to apportion blame or liability for something that happens in the business. This could be financial, or could be even more serious, when an accident happens and someone gets hurt.

In the circumstances of a court battle it is quite possible that a judge will, in assessing blame, look at board minutes behind the business decision. And in doing so they will not be looking with hindsight at whether the decision was right or wrong. Instead their focus will be on whether the decision was reasonable and reached after appropriate consideration of all the material factors.

Image: www.unsplash.com - Austin Distel

The logic is that most decisions are not black and white with an obvious 'correct' answer. They are nearly always decisions based on balancing pros and cons and deciding the best way forward.

Things do, in the real world, go wrong and judges are NOT business people so are not there to second guess the decision. They are there to assess whether the board made an appropriate decision after proper and diligent consideration of the factors involved or whether the board was negligent. Board minutes are key in enabling them to answer that question.

If the minutes don't mention that due diligence then the judge could decide the board didn't do its job and so was negligent in making the decision without proper consideration. And on the contrary if the minutes, or an accompanying board paper, show that a full set of risks and challenges were considered and on balance the board decided to progress because they were outweighed by the benefits, then even if subsequently things go wrong, the judge may well conclude the board had done what could reasonably be expected of them in an uncertain and unpredictable world.

Image: www.unsplash.com - Bernd Klutsch

Board papers

Which leads to a final comment; note the reference to board papers. The preparation of board papers is very helpful in enabling clear and precise decisions and in keeping minutes simple.

So preparing high quality board papers to support a recommendation for a board decision is a great help both in making better, more informed, decisions and also in demonstrating (by attaching them to the minutes) that the board had made those decisions with appropriate due diligence.

In summary

Minutes are important because they provide a written record of the decisions made by a board and the actions delegated to management in pursuit of those decisions. Most importantly they document the deliberations of the board and can be used to support or refute allegations of negligence.

Well-written minutes reflect positively on both the company and its directors, and play an important role in protecting directors from personal liability.

Image: www.canva.com

Appendix J
The 4-box report

A reporting format I was introduced to many years ago and like - for its brevity and clarity - is what I call a 4-box report. I've used it for many years when wanting Directors and Project Managers to report progress formally to a meeting.

The first benefit is that the report is on one page / one slide. This constrains the level of detail to an amount that is useful - at least at a headline level. If essential an item can be backed up by a detailed report and certainly I would expect important headlines to be explained in the meeting.

The second benefit is that the four boxes make clear what the item is dealing with. Differentiating clearly between reporting factually the past (on the left) and communicating about the expected future (on the right). And likewise differentiating between achievements and goals (at the top) and problems and risks (at the bottom).

Image: www.canva.com

The end report typically looks like this (a real but anonymised example):

Period ending 8th May	**Milestones achieved:** • New brochures well received and new PDFs created for emailing purposes • A5 leaflet produced for lead generation in local PC stores; cafes ;newsagents etc • Leaflet holder also ordered to hold leaflets in place • Highest ever number of sales achieved in one week 34 - previous highest 28 • Total NSV £266k vs budget £311k	**Problems encountered and impact:** • Significant drop in leads has left the pot very low Predictive dialler has been ceased short term • 1 member of team given extended probationary period given to see if it 'cuts the mustard' • Recruit planned to replace Gurminder did not turn up - so still recruiting.
Next period to 5th June	**Milestones to be achieved:** • PDFs for desktop versions • A5 leaflet to be produced for telesales lead generation • Revamp of secondary lead brochure • One week exhibition in Brooksway shopping centre 28th May - 2nd June • Look at deferred decision quotes to see if we can resuscitate any sales	**Challenges and risks to be managed:** • Two staff short against plan • Impact of time spent on training new team • Maintaining level of motivation within team and gain every sale we can out of the leads we have • Highest sales week 1st week in May but lowest average NSV ytd in same week of year

Checklists

Checklist
First week

- [ ] No two businesses, even direct competitors in the same industry, are ever the same. They may have different ownership, structures, ambitions, leadership and most importantly cultures and market position
- [ ] Use your first meeting to set the tone of your leadership. Signal your style and that you are engaging and open but in control
- [ ] Priority is to settle in. Find your desk, meet your immediate reports and explain your working style and your immediate priorities
- [ ] Unless you have some previous insight or the organisation is in crisis, this is not a time for decisions – at least not for finally committing to them and communicating them
- [ ] Establish why you are there. Why have you been appointed?
- [ ] Research perceptions of the business from all angles. Where do the people involved in the business feel they are? Use your newness to your advantage. Play dumb. Ask dumb questions. How does this work? Why do we do this? How do we feel about that?
- [ ] Meet all staff individually in small groups or sample groups depending upon the scale of the organisation - one of the biggest motivators of staff is being asked their opinion and being listened to. And you can get powerful insights into the state of the business

Checklist
First month: Weeks 2-4

- [ ] Use this moment to build a personal and practical relationship, business leader to business leader, with the most senior contact you can reach within your top customers

- [ ] Meet and understand customers - hear directly from them about their experiences with your company. Get a good understanding of your customers' needs and how you can better serve then

- [ ] Review the customer journey encompassing all the touchpoints and experiences that a customer has with your business, from start to finish. Especially engaging with the people actually doing the activities on a day to day basis.

- [ ] Ensure you have a good handle on how the organisation actually progresses potential customers from being unaware to being satisfied, repeat customers.

- [ ] Meet suppliers. Assess the state of the relationship. How well does your business work with them at the moment? Is there a clear and transparent relationship and a mutual understanding of how you help each other succeed?

- [ ] Meet stakeholders. Once you've explored the perceptions and priorities of staff, customers and suppliers it is a good time for you to check back and reassess their priorities. Confirm why am I here?

- [ ] Examine the strategic opportunities. How can you deliver more, better and more profitable products and services to your customers utilising their supply line. And meeting them is also a good chance to understand their perspective of your industry.
- [ ] Be positive and upbeat but be yourself and honest
- [ ] Reflect on what they said before making critical decisions

Image: www.freepik.com

Play your leadership cards right

Bob Bradley

Checklist
First 'month': Week 5

- [ ] Take some time away from the routine at this stage. Clarify your thoughts and what you've learnt throughout the first month. "Far too many people get weighed down in doing, and never take the time to think and feel"

- [ ] Consider your company's purpose. By starting with the 'Why' or the purpose, cause or belief that drives a business, leaders can inspire people (both staff and customers) to take action and create a loyal following

- [ ] Define your market precisely. Make sure you are very clear on the characteristics that define your customer and, if B2B, the role and persona / personality of the key buyer within the customer business

- [ ] Make sure you are clear on how your business creates value for your customer. How do you help them to be more successful? Why do they buy?

- [ ] Understand your business model. What is your channel to market that allows you to reach them efficiently? Who are your key suppliers and what is your supply chain? What is your process and business model that allows you to reach them and serve them profitably?

- [ ] Be clear too on your market position. Precisely why do customers buy from you specifically?

- [ ] At this stage it's critical to have role clarity. A clear definition of who is responsible for what, is important so people don't spend time conflicting and treading on each others' toes, or arguing about whose fault it was when things go wrong because activities, responsibilities and functions are unclear or incomplete

- [ ] Whilst you need to decide (and agree with stakeholders) the overall direction, you need the team to succeed to make it happen. You can't cover every detail. Your critical success factor at this point is your choice of projects and your choice of people to lead them

- [ ] How does the organisation communicate? When designing the communication processes be very clear of the purpose of each meeting; daily, weekly, monthly and beyond

- [ ] Expectations of you will be high so there will be pressure to be ambitious. But knowledge of your new company is limited so keep an eye on budgets and financials. Maybe have a conversation budget (which you MUST achieve or exceed) and a target that is a stretch but believe you can achieve

Image: www.freepik.com - aopsan

Checklist
First month: 'Week 6'

- [ ] Ensure your plans have the backing of critical players
- [ ] Plan the launch, along with outlining the process and sequence of communication. Note that sequence is very important. (including the external communication plan)
- [ ] If restructuring, pose the question to yourself - "Do I genuinely believe that the restructuring I am leading is in the best interests of the business and sustaining (or re-establishing) its success in the future?" If that isn't the case then you need to look in the mirror and ask yourself why are you doing it?
- [ ] Get your first key messages absolutely clear in your head. A first key message for the majority of the staff is likely to be to acknowledge that change isn't always easy and whilst necessary to protect the business and achieve the vision, may be disruptive and painful for some.
- [ ] Think about how your communication is going to differ between continuing staff and staff that may be leaving

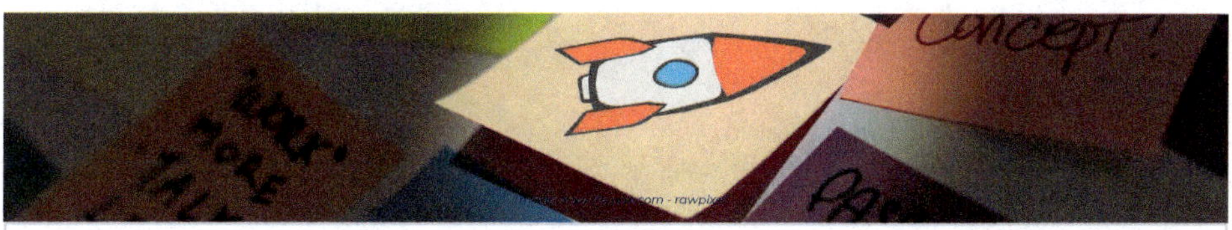

Checklist
First quarter: Weeks 7-14

- [ ] Deliver the quick wins fast so you have the credibility to drive through the bigger and longer projects
- [ ] Kick off and deliver the major projects while you are new and listened to. Momentum is important!
- [ ] Communicate your progress and goals achieved weekly with credit and positive reinforcement to those doing the great work of delivering change
- [ ] However much work you put in, you can't know everything in your planning phase and get everything right. So get going, head in roughly the right direction and then quickly adjust as you learn
- [ ] Right" does not always mean perfect. To a customer "right" includes the dimensions of "When I need it" and "At a price I can afford". So to spend too long producing a product after the customer has gone elsewhere or that is too perfect and therefore too expensive is not "Right" for the (ex) customer
- [ ] "To go faster, go slower" - this reflects the conflict a good leader has to reconcile to achieve optimum results. To deliver products or services that operate to the level of performance needed, at the time needed, within the budget needed, by their chosen market
- [ ] Review progress with your management team. Identify, highlight, celebrate and promote things that have gone well and to learn from what hasn't

Checklist
First year

☐ Life as a leader is never and should never become normal. Good leadership is always about change. Change as a result of learning and understanding. Identifying where and how the business can be better and developing the capability of the team to do more and more

☐ Finally, get outside the business and look for opportunities to use your success to do more, better. To grow the business, serve more customers, solve even more of the challenges of the world, make it a better place and by doing so earn a decent living for yourselves and your funders

Image: www.freepik.com

The author: Bob Bradley
The business leader for business leaders

The author: Bob Bradley
The business leader for business leaders

I am lucky to have had such a broad career in business leadership built upon the solid foundation of great academic credentials.

I have led six businesses as General manager, Managing Director or Chief Executive. Earlier in my career I led departments, business units and projects. I was responsible for selling and leading numerous corporate transformation projects worth £1M+ as well as leading a division of a well known business consultancy specialising in Hypergrowth businesses.

Three of the businesses I ran were small and I was the owner of two. Three more businesses were medium sized with up to **£50M revenues** and **500 staff**. In all three cases I was appointed to address slowing or declining revenues and enable growth. Of the three larger businesses I ran, one was a corporate subsidiary, one an **AIM listed** business and one a **family** business.

I have led the integration of businesses following mergers six times and completed two acquisitions from start to finish.

I have been on **19** boards, ten of them commercial, and seven not for profit.

I have created and chaired three trusts, one an **employee ownership (EO) trust**, the others in the public sector. I was a **National Leader of Governance** for the Department for Education and have twice been a board advisor guiding the governance of a small enterprise.

I have facilitated over **800** meetings of business leaders, roughly half of them online and the rest in person and engaged in close confidential conversation about business challenges with over **300** different business leaders. I have arranged and hosted over **500** workshops with over **200** different professional speakers.

Today?

I am semi-retired because whilst I have exited my own business and no longer have an operational leadership role I remain passionate about **practical leadership of real operational businesses.**

I learnt so much the hard way myself and then so much more from all the business leaders I worked with.

Contributing to their debates about the real challenges they faced in their businesses has given me so many **INSIGHTS** into how real, practical operational business leaders **think, decide and act.** Insights I wish I'd had forty years ago. Insights I feel it's my duty to share as widely as possible!

My beliefs and values about business

Today's world is a VUCA world. It is volatile, uncertain, complex and ambiguous.

It conspires to confuse and behave unpredictably. We should (as an academic called Nassim Nicholas Taleb and a popular journalist called Tim Harford) suggest, stop trying to predict and forecast and plan so much.

Rather than try to plan for all outcomes, and find the one that happens is the one we didn't plan for, we need to increase the number of tools we have in our toolbag so we can cope with whatever happens.

My belief

We need to focus our efforts on building resilience and the ability to adapt. In ourselves and our business. So we cope and our businesses survive and thrive whatever.

I encourage you to spend less time developing complex long term plans, on spreadsheets, on forecasting and on planning and budgeting and more time on learning how to deal with whatever life throws at you.

My learning

I've learnt that business doesn't need to be complicated. The best businesses, the best leaders and the best decisions generally share the characteristic of being clear and simple.

My broader beliefs and values about leadership and the purpose of business and enterprise

Business should be a force for good in the world, creating value by solving challenges the world faces. Solving them so well that its customers are pleased to pass a fair share of that value on to the business.

The business in turn shares fairly that value between its staff, its investors and funders, its suppliers and its wider community.

(Where the term business includes all forms of enterprise private, public and third sector as the purpose of all should be to create value and share it fairly.)

Leaders make a difference. The person who has the greatest impact on the extent to which an organisation creates value is the leader of that organisation.

Leadership is a learning journey. None of us is the finished article - the perfect leader. However good a leader we are, we can always be even better. We succeed or we learn. We get things right - and we succeed.

We make mistakes - and we learn. Whatever happens we become an even better leader. We learn from experience!

We can learn quicker. By being hungry for ideas from fellow leaders, specialists, experts and thinkers. By sharing best practice and learning from the experience of diverse others. Learning from their successes and their mistakes and they learning from ours.

We are stronger together. Sharing journeys. Comparing experiences. Learning from successes and mistakes. Supporting and challenging. Helping each other to be the best we can be.

We are individual leaders. Equal but different. People of varying genders, races, backgrounds, education, physical and mental characteristics. Leaders at different stages of our career with varying personalities, attitudes, beliefs, values and goals. We have different types of leadership role and operate within a variety of ownership structures and ownership ambitions. Our organisations are at different stages of development targeting different purposes with differing business models in a range of sectors and geographies.

We are all though equal - all peers. Striving to be the best leader we can be. Striving to run the best and most successful business we can.

Printed in Great Britain
by Amazon

61489198R00067